How To
PROSPECT,
SELL and BUILD

YOUR NETWORK
MARKETING BUSINESS

WITH *STORIES*

TOM "BIG AL" SCHREITER

For information, contact:

Fortune Network Publishing
PO Box 890084
Houston, TX 77289 USA
Telephone: +1 (281) 280-9800

ISBN: 1-892366-18-5
ISBN-13: 978-1-892366-18-4

DEDICATION

This book is dedicated to network marketers everywhere.

I travel the world 240+ days each year. Let me know if you want me to stop in your area and conduct a live Big Al training.

http://www.BigAlSeminars.com

Get 7 mini-reports of amazing, easy sentences that create new, hot prospects.

Sign up today at:
http://www.BigAlReport.com

Other great Big Al Books available at:

http://www.BigAlBooks.com

Table of Contents

PREFACE

History remembers great storytellers.

Why? Because they were the best communicators.

And isn't that the skill network marketers need most? To communicate the message inside of our heads ... and get it inside our prospects' heads so that they see what we see.

These are the stories I use to communicate to prospects and network marketers. Some of the stories are so old that the origin of the original composer is hard to trace.

If you wish to join the elite builders in network marketing, just remember this phrase:

"Facts tell. Stories sell."

So I won't spend much time explaining how stories work in this book. Instead, I'll just share stories.

-- Tom "Big Al" Schreiter

It Is Not What We Say,
It Is What People Hear That Matters.

We have to influence people to **believe** us. Not preach. Not lecture. Not educate. We have to get past our prospects' negativity, their bad programs, their sales resistance, their skepticism ... and that is easy to do.

With a **story**.

* Stories don't set up sales resistance.

* Stories are easily remembered.

* Stories get people to act.

* People are programmed to listen to stories.

* Stories talk to the prospect's subconscious mind.

* And stories are fun to listen to.

To be more professional, all we have to do is stop doing fact-filled presentations and simply put our information inside of a story. Remember, "It is not what we say, it is what people hear that matters."

Stories are the best way to communicate to prospects. They are fast, efficient, and prospects "get it" quickly. In fact, a simple short story could replace your entire business presentation. Really?

Yes. Let's take a look at sponsoring young people. Instead of a long presentation about residual income, compensation percentages, incredible research, and other boring items, let's just get to the point and get our young prospect to make an immediate decision to join our business. How? With a better story, of course. And the story doesn't have to be long. Let's try this.

The Ukraine Story.

I was talking to a group of distributors in the Ukraine. Maybe I was the youngest person in the room, and hey, I'm old! So I asked the group,

"So what did you say to keep all the young people away?"

Apparently these Ukrainians didn't have a sense of humor. They were angry. They yelled, "What do you mean we said something to keep the young people away?"

So I asked them, "Well, what did you say to the young prospects?"

Their reply? "We told them they could retire ten years early with our wonderful opportunity!"

***

Well, to an 18-year-old, retiring ten years early isn't very motivating. The Ukrainians were telling the wrong story. If I was talking to younger people in the United States, maybe I would use the following story:

Ted and Rick.

Ted graduates from university and starts his climb up the corporate ladder. Every day he works long hours. He spends Saturday on projects to try to get ahead. No time for sports, no time for relationships, and no money to save. Every month he reviews his goals to see how far he can climb the corporate ladder. Extra meetings, extra projects. Gradually, Ted begins his climb to the top. And after 18 short years, Ted has his chance. He could become the next new, semi-young, chief executive of the company. But the owner gives the chief executive job to his recently graduated grandson, who promptly fires Ted.

Ted has lost 18 years of his life, his dignity, his hard effort, and is again unemployed.

Ted's friend, Rick, also leaves university, but takes an ordinary job. However, Rick does something different. In the evenings, after work, Rick starts his part-time network marketing business. Four years later, Rick fires his boss, and lives the rest of his life on the earnings of his network marketing business.

***

That was simple. In just a few words a younger person understands that working a business now can pay off later. We didn't have to convince anyone, sell anyone, or plead our case.

Because these were stories, they were readily accepted into our prospects' minds. We didn't have to fight to get our message inside our prospects' heads.

I joined network marketing because of a story. I am a "green" personality, very analytical. Yet, it was the story that sold me. Here is what happened.

I answered an ad in the newspaper and came to a Saturday morning opportunity meeting. It lasted three hours! And boy, was it strange.

In the room, 150 people were cheering. They looked like a bunch of anti-government communist hippies. The meeting talked about how they were cleansing the body, how strange stuff came out of their colons, and how they wanted to break from the 40-year plan.

I would have left early, but they had armed guards at the back of the room. Finally, after three grueling hours, the meeting ended. As I sneaked out of the back of the room, one man stopped me and said, "Are you the person who answered my ad?"

How did he know? Later I found out I was the only guest. The rest were all distributors already.

So I answered, "Yes, I answered your ad. But I'm not interested. I listened to the entire meeting. It is not for me." After three hours of facts, I said, "No."

But here is the power of a story. All my sponsor did was to tell me a little story. It took only about **30 seconds**. At the end of the story I said, "So how do I join?"

Get it? Three hours of facts, no sale. Only a 30-second story, I joined.

That's the power of the story. Would you like to know the story he told me? Here it is.

Fire the Boss.

"Big Al, when you join our business, here is what happens. Six months from now you walk into your boss' office. You sit down in the chair, you put your feet up on his desk and you leave little scuff marks with your heels.

"Then you put your hands behind your head and you calmly tell the boss that you can't fit him into your schedule any longer. You've enjoyed working there, but if they have any problems after you leave, they can call you any Tuesday morning at 11:00 a.m. at your normal consulting rate.

"Then you get up from the boss' office, walk out to the main office desk, pick up your personal belongings, wave good-bye to all your fellow workers who said it couldn't be done, hop into your brand-new bonus car, drive down to the drive-in teller window, deposit this month's bonus check, and say to the bank teller:

"'Oh, I don't know. Put this bonus check in savings or checking. It really doesn't matter. I get these checks every month.'

"And then you drive home and relax, and have a nice glass of your favorite beverage."

***

At the end of that story I said, "So how do I join?"

Wouldn't you have liked to enroll me into your network marketing program? Well, if you used facts, PowerPoint, videos, flip charts and research reports ... you would have failed. It was a story that got me started in network marketing.

Successful networkers are great storytellers. Most of the top leaders are great storytellers. Shouldn't you become a great storyteller?

Stories Can Be Really Short.

Sometimes we talk too long and our presentations trigger objections. One objection that scares new distributors is the pyramid objection.

Usually the pyramid objection really isn't about the prospect worrying about being in an illegal pyramid. Instead, this is just a convenient objection the prospect uses to stop a long-winded presentation.

But let's imagine someone says, "Isn't this a pyramid?"

Here is how network marketing pro Robert Butwin answers that objection. He uses a story that changes the entire direction of the conversation. Here is what he says.

It Is a Pyramid!

"Before I answer your question, is it okay if I ask you a quick question?

"When you were getting your formal education at school, if your teachers would have received a small percentage of your earnings for the rest of your life, do you think your formal education would have been better?"

The prospect answers, "Of course."

Robert continues, "Well, that is how network marketing works. Your sponsor wants to teach and train you to be as successful as possible, because the only way your sponsor can earn money is by making you successful."

***

And with this simple, short story, the objection goes away and is replaced with a benefit.

Food for Thought.

One married couple goes out to a restaurant twice a week for dinner. They spend $160 a month on eating out. They get fat.

Another married couple invests $160 a month in their own network marketing business. They stay slim and healthy. In a few years they retire.

***

I like this short story. It opens up the prospects' minds and lets them know that a small change of behavior can make them successful.

Also, when I use this story, I don't get the objection, "I can't afford it." They are already spending the money they need to participate in their own network marketing business. Now it is a matter of choice. Do they want to continue to dine out or would they rather eventually own the restaurant?

How does network marketing really work? It is best described in a story.

The Grocery Store.

Imagine I go to the local grocery store and buy a diet soda and 44 candy bars. I pay for these items and I leave.

You are right behind me in line and you buy a diet soda and 44 candy bars. You pay for these items, but just before you leave, you show your loyalty card. The local grocery store then gives you some free bonus points so you can eventually go to Hawaii.

Well, that's how network marketing works. We both do exactly the same thing, but you get something extra. A trip to Hawaii.

But it gets even better. The local grocery store calls you up and says,

"Hey, I see you've been using your loyalty card. We like giving you points. Please tell your neighbors about our loyalty card so they come and shop here also. When your neighbors come and shop here, we will give them their own loyalty card. Now, every time they buy groceries, we will give them their bonus points so they can go to Hawaii with you. And, for helping us out and letting your neighbors know about our loyalty card, every time we give your neighbors some bonus points, we are going to give you some extra bonus points too so that you can go to Hawaii a lot sooner."

Well that's how network marketing works, except we don't give bonus points, we give cash.

***

At the end of the story prospects say, "Well, yeah, makes sense." And you've changed their whole belief about network marketing.

Use your imagination. You could use this same type of story to describe airline loyalty programs.

Prospects Are Scared.

Every prospect wants what network marketing offers, but yet they hesitate. Why? The fear of the unknown, the fear of failure, and the fear of what others will say if they are unsuccessful. These three fears keep many prospects from getting started.

A simple story can relieve those fears so our prospects can join, learn and benefit from our network marketing business. Let's look at more sample stories.

The New Machine.

Imagine you are sitting at your desk at work and the boss comes to you and gives you this proposal.

"We just bought a new machine for the company and we need to train someone to operate this new machine. You would have to go to night school three days a week for nine months to learn how to operate this machine. We wouldn't pay you for going to night school, but when you graduated from night school, you would be our machine operator and you would get a $1,500 per month raise. What do you think?"

Most people would reply, "Yes! I could spend three nights a week for nine months in training so that I could get a $1,500 a month raise."

And isn't that what your network marketing opportunity offers? If you really dedicated yourself, three nights a week for nine months, you should have enough distributors and customers to easily earn $1,500 extra per month.

Now, your current job doesn't offer the opportunity to work three nights a week and get a huge raise, but our network marketing opportunity does.

***

Stories help us communicate better. Stories can provide examples that our prospect can relate to. Here is a longer story that also helps scared prospects.

Good News and Bad News.

Imagine for a moment that you are sitting at your desk at your job. The boss comes up to you, taps you on the shoulder and says, "I've got some good news and I've got some bad news."

You reply, "I am brave. Give me the bad news first."

The boss says, "Well, the bad news is, you are fired."

You are thinking, "Whoa, that is bad news. Oh, that is really, really bad news. If I get fired, I have to go home and tell my spouse I got fired, and that would be pretty embarrassing. What if I can't find another job for a year? Or what if the new job doesn't pay as much or what if the new job is far away and I have to fight traffic when I commute? What if the people are mean at my new job? Oh, this is really, really bad news!"

You panic and say to your boss, "Oh my goodness, this is terribly bad news. So what is the good news?"

The boss replies, "Well the good news is, you have the rest of the afternoon off."

Now you have a full-scale panic attack. "Arrgh! Oh no! I don't want to be fired. Is there any way you can keep me?"

The boss says, "Well, we outsourced most of our jobs, so we could only keep a few people. If you want to be one of the people we keep on staff, you would have to agree to work one hour of overtime every day for free, Monday through Friday, from 5:00 pm to 6:00 pm. If you worked that one hour of free overtime every day, we could afford to keep you."

Like most hard-working people with family and debt obligations, you say, "Yes, I will work that overtime so I can keep my job."

The boss smiles. "Great. Thanks for being a team player. I know the extra hour of overtime is a sacrifice, but since you are a team player and are willing to help us in these tough times, let me tell you what our company is going to do for you.

"If you work your regular hours and this overtime for the next two years, at the end of those two years the company will let you retire at full pay."

Now what are you thinking? Jackpot! This is the best day of your life, right? You are thinking, "Wow, all I have to do is work one hour of free overtime five days a week, and in just two years I can retire at full pay."

Exciting!

You rush home to tell your spouse about this fantastic offer. And you start working the one free hour of overtime daily for about six months.

Then, you are at a party. Some friends make fun of you and say, "Oh man, look at you. You are just so stupid. You work an hour of overtime every day for free. The company is taking advantage of you. Quit that terrible job and get a job where they will pay you for every hour you work."

What would you say?

"No, no, no. I am not quitting this job. I only have 18 more months of working one free hour of overtime every day, and then I can quit and retire forever!"

So you continue working this one free hour of overtime for 18 months. Only six more months to go. That night you come home and your spouse says, "You know what dear? We miss you for dinner when you work overtime. Quit that job, get a new job where you can come home an hour earlier for dinner."

What would you say?

"No way, only six months to go and I can retire at full pay."

You would continue working this one free hour of overtime for the full two years, and then the company would let you retire at full pay.

Wouldn't that be awesome?

Now unfortunately, your job doesn't offer that benefit. **But we do.**

When you join our network marketing business, we are going to ask you to work your new business just one hour every day, Monday through Friday, **talking to people.**

Your one hour is not moving pixels on a computer screen, not playing pen pal all night, not surfing the web ... but talking to "live" people.

If you talk to "live" people for just one hour every day, Monday through Friday, at the end of two years, you will have enough customers and distributors on your team to equal your current full-time income and you can retire at full pay.

Now, I know what you're thinking. You are thinking, "Well, I would like this to happen, I would like to try, but I don't know what to say to people."

Well, of course you don't know what to say to people. You haven't learned any skills yet, but you will learn as you go. You could learn to do anything in an hour a day for two years, couldn't you? You could even learn to play the piano by practicing an hour a day for two years.

So maybe the first week in our business, you learn to say, "Hi."

During week number two, you learn to say, "My name is ____."

You would get better every week. And at the end of two years, you could retire at full pay. So what do you think?

***

What do you think a lot of people would say to this story?

"Sign me up!"

Now, pause for a moment and think about this. The prospects would say, "Sign me up," and they haven't even heard the name of your company yet.

This should prove to anyone that it is not about the company, the products, the compensation plan, etc. It is all about the story you tell.

But this story does so much more.

You have upgraded your prospect from someone who just wanted to try the business, or someone who just wanted to earn his distributor kit money back ... to someone who is willing to work for two years at no pay! Wow, now that is a pretty good prospect.

By the way, when this prospect joins, he will probably get some bonus checks quickly. Remember, he is expecting to work two years for free. What are you going to say to him when his first bonus check arrives?

You could say, "It's a mistake, just give it to me, I will send it back for you." Just kidding. But wouldn't that first bonus check be a great surprise along your new distributor's two-year journey?

Want another short story for scared prospects?

New prospects fear joining our business. Who should they talk to? What will happen if people reject them or make fun of them? What if they fail? What will their friends say if they made a mistake?

The fear of the unknown is huge. Prospects want to join our business, but they also want to feel safe from failure.

Here is a story that lets your prospect know that it is okay to have that fear, and that you will help him be successful.

The Mice and the Cat.

Once upon a time, there was a house with lots of mice. They were fat and happy. One day a cat moved in. The mice had a meeting. "What should we do? The cat will eat us! Every day that cat sneaks up behind us and chases us back into our holes."

Finally they decided on a brilliant solution. They would put a bell around the cat's neck, so whenever they heard the bell, they could rush into their holes before the cat could eat them.

Then one mouse said to the others, "The solution is excellent. Put a bell around the cat's neck. But the real question is: who is going to put the bell around the cat's neck?"

The moral of the story is that we all know **what** we need to do (join and get started), but there is great fear in **doing** it.

I know you want to start or build a business. Would it be okay if I helped you get started by putting the bell around the cat's neck and then you can say good-bye to fear?

***

How do you think your new prospect feels now? Do you think he feels good about you, an experienced professional, helping the new prospect get started and removing the unknown?

But you could also tell the "Restaurant Story" to make your prospect feel good, and to assure your prospect that the business can be learned as we go.

The Restaurant.

The prospect was scared to join.

He said, "But I don't know how to start a network marketing business. I don't know anything about the products, the compensation plan is too hard to explain, and I don't know how to talk to people. Who would I talk to? I don't know how to do this!"

The sponsor reassured his prospect. "Do you know anything about running a restaurant?"

"No."

The sponsor continued. "Let's say you wanted to open your own restaurant, but wanted to do it slowly. You aren't sure you can handle it, so you decide to open only one day a week, Friday. You won't take any risks. Your restaurant will be strictly part-time, open only two hours on Friday evenings."

The scared prospect replied, "I could feel comfortable with that."

The sponsor continued his story. "To make things easier, you should allow customers to come by invitation only. You don't want too many on your first night. I will help you for the first couple of Fridays."

"So far this sounds easy enough." The scared prospect was starting to relax a bit.

"We'll invite just four of your friends for opening night. You and I will serve their meals. If they like the food, we'll ask them to tell others. How does that sound so far?"

"Sounds fair." The scared prospect was starting to lean forward.

"The next Friday night, we will allow each of your four friends to bring one new guest. Now we have 8 customers. You and I have last week's experience under our belt, so we should be a little better now, right?"

"Sure. Eight people wouldn't be any problem for you and me." The prospect was now getting more confident.

"The next Friday night, we will allow each of our eight customers to bring one additional guest. Now we have 16 guests to serve. We still plan to be open only two hours and keep this business part-time, so maybe we'll expand to another night. We don't want more than 16 guests at a time."

"That makes sense." The prospect was now smiling.

"Let's expand to Tuesday nights. We'll hire our most enthusiastic customer as an assistant and begin to train him to do the same. To make sure our Friday night stays easy to operate, we'll send some of our customers to our assistant who will do Tuesday nights. This will help Tuesdays start with a bang."

The prospect took control. "I'm getting the picture. I can learn as I go. Maybe network marketing won't be so hard if I go one step at a time. Sign me up. Let's start inviting my four guests for my Friday night opportunity meeting."

***

So why don't prospects believe they can start their own successful part-time network marketing business?

I'm sure you have heard prospects say:

"Oh, that will never work."

Why do your prospects automatically say this when presented with a business opportunity? Because they have been conditioned by:

- Their parents who told them to get a good job to succeed in life.

- Their school teachers who told them to get good grades so that they can get a worthwhile career job.

- Their friends who told them that they should just fit in with everyone else.

- The newspaper and television reporters who have full-time jobs.

The easiest explanation is with a story.

The Ape Story.

Start with a cage containing five apes. In the cage, hang a banana on a string and put stairs under it. Before long, an ape will go to the stairs and start to climb towards the banana. As soon as he touches the stairs, spray all of the apes with cold water.

After a while, another ape makes an attempt with the same result - all the apes are sprayed with cold water.

Turn off the cold water.

Later, if another ape tries to climb the stairs, the other apes will try to prevent it, **even though no water sprays them**.

Now, remove one ape from the cage and replace it with a new ape.

The new ape sees the banana and wants to climb the stairs. To his horror, all of the other apes attack him.

After another attempt and attack, the ape knows that if he tries to climb the stairs, he will be assaulted.

Next, remove another of the original five apes and replace it with a new ape. The new ape goes to the stairs and is attacked. The previous new ape takes part in the punishment with enthusiasm. Again, replace a third original ape with a new one. The new one makes it to the stairs and is attacked as well.

Two of the four apes that beat him have no idea why they were not permitted to climb the stairs, or why they are participating in the beating of the newest ape.

After replacing the fourth and fifth original apes, all of the original apes that were sprayed with cold water have been replaced.

Nevertheless, no ape ever again approaches the stairs. Why not?

"Because that's the way it's always been around here."

Yes, our prospects sometimes use this same irrational thinking to reject an opportunity to change their lives.

It Doesn't Take Big Checks
To Motivate People To Join.

Would $300 a month make a difference in someone's lifestyle? It sure could. And, it might even take less than that to excite someone to join. Here are a couple of stories using smaller income projections that prospects can relate to.

The $50 Payoff.

I know of one instance where a $50 monthly bonus check made all the difference in the world for one distributor. I had lunch with the young man several years ago. He was a vegetable farmer from Missouri. When his $50 bonus check arrived in the mail, he was so excited he couldn't stop talking about it. I couldn't figure out why, so I asked him, "Why all this excitement over a $50 bonus check?"

He answered, "You see, I'm a vegetable farmer. After all my expenses, I end up with about $5 a month that I can call my own. That's it. Just $5. Well, I got this $50 bonus check, and that's 10 times more spending money that I usually have. I can take the family to a movie or have dinner out. I have at least a dozen different choices I've never had before."

***

He got me thinking. If your regular job pays all your day-to-day expenses, then any bonus check you receive for your part-time business is "fun money." It's not spoken for. So, if you have an extra $500 bonus check each month, WOW! You could use it to make payments on a brand-new car. Or, get a larger house. Or, take a cruise every two or three months. Or, set up an investment program and retire early. Use your imagination. Hmmm. Extra money really means more once your everyday expenses are covered by your salary.

The $100,000 Problem.

Sometimes the part-time bonus checks even exceed your full-time salary.

My good friend, Tom, had a problem. His regular job earned him $50,000 a year. After working his network marketing business part-time for three years, his part-time network marketing bonus income neared $100,000 a year. Now, I wouldn't think he had a problem, but he came to me with a worried face and said, "Tom, I'm just getting too busy. I'm afraid I won't be able to service both my job and my part-time business fairly, unless I give up one of them. I like giving good service and doing things first-class."

Well, my friend had good network marketing skills and his part-time income certainly was impressive, but I really questioned his business sense.

I said, "If you are making twice as much part-time in network marketing as your full-time salary, I think it would make sense to quit your full-time job and enjoy your $100,000 part-time income."

He agreed. Now his part-time network marketing income continues to increase and he has time to work out at the gym, spend time with his family, visit with friends on the telephone, travel, and yes, he still fits in his network marketing business.

***

While he may have been confused originally on which career to give up, it does prove that you don't have to be a nuclear scientist to build large incomes in network marketing.

The Conservative Approach.

Another friend, Bob, used a conservative investment strategy to build a fortune from a relatively modest network marketing monthly bonus check of only $500.

How did he do it?

He said to himself, "My monthly paycheck from my regular job pays all of my bills, so I'll just use the extra $500 a month to pay off my house mortgage faster." In only four years' time his house was completely paid off. Now, he had an extra $1,000 a month free because there were no more mortgage payments, plus the additional $500 a month network marketing bonus check.

With the $1,500 extra monthly spendable cash, where should he invest it?

Bob purchased the house next door. The tenants' rent payment paid the monthly mortgage. Bob invested the extra $1,500 of his monthly cash flow to accelerate his mortgage repayment schedule. In about five years, the house next door was completely debt-free.

Now Bob's financial picture looked like this. His regular job paid all his living expenses, plus he had $1,000 a month free because he had no mortgage on his personal residence. Rental income from the house next door added an additional $1,000 of monthly cash flow. And, Bob's bonus check still averaged an extra $500 a month. So what did Bob do with his extra $2,500 in extra cash flow?

He purchased another house down the street. The tenants' rent paid the monthly mortgage, plus Bob added an additional $2,500 a month in principal reduction.

Soon Bob's financial picture looked like this. His regular job paid all his living expenses, plus he had $1,000 a month free because he had no mortgage on his personal residence. Rental income from the house next door added an additional $1,000 of monthly cash flow. Rental income from the house down the street added an additional $1,000 of monthly cash flow. And, Bob's bonus check still averaged an extra $500 a month. So what did Bob do with his extra $3,500 in extra cash flow?

Well, you get the picture. Bob never earned more than an average $500 bonus check, yet now, he is financially secure. Even if Bob lost his job and his network marketing company went out of business, his monthly rental collections would support him nicely. As of today, his monthly net income is over $5,000 from rental payments alone.

***

Most People Do Network Marketing Every Day, But They Just Don't Get Paid For It.

Network marketing is **recommending** and promoting the things you like to other people.

We do this activity almost every day. Networking is a natural skill that everyone **already** possesses! In network marketing, we simply collect residual income checks for doing what we do every day.

How about a couple of examples of daily networking?

Check out those dinosaurs!

One of my favorite movies is *Jurassic Park*. This 1993 movie was a breakthrough with the digital dinosaurs looking very real. I think a few other people liked that movie too, as it is one of the best-selling movies of all time.

Imagine you are sitting across the kitchen table talking with one of your friends. Your friend says,

"Network marketing? I don't know about that. I probably couldn't do it."

Why does your friend say that?

Because your friend doesn't really know what network marketing is. Your friend thinks it might require selling, presentation skills, knowing vast amounts of motivated salespeople, or some other similar misconception.

Your friend is making an uneducated decision based on inadequate facts.

Your job is to give your friend the facts about network marketing.

Then, your friend is free to make a decision to join, or not to join, based upon accurate information.

You might use the *Jurassic Park* movie to illustrate how network marketing really works. The conversation could go something like this:

You: Have you ever seen the movie, *Jurassic Park*?

Friend: Yeah, it was great.

You: When you went to see the movie, did you purchase a ticket and did you get some snacks at the snack bar (at value pricing)?

Friend: Sure did. Actually the snacks were kind of expensive, but I really like their popcorn.

You: After watching the movie, did you keep it top secret? Or, did you tell a friend about it?

Friend: As soon as I returned home, I called my sister and told her that she and her husband **had** to see *Jurassic Park*. It was a-w-e-s-o-m-e! The Dolby stereo made the seats shake, just as if the dinosaurs were walking next to you.

You: Did your sister and her husband go see Jurassic Park because of your recommendation?

Friend: You bet! They got a ticket for that evening's showing.

You: So they purchased tickets and probably got some snacks too, right?

Friend: Yes, and they loved the movie. My sister's husband is a lawyer, so she loved the part where the dinosaur eats the lawyer while the lawyer is well, uh, on the toilet.

You: Did your sister and her husband tell anyone else about *Jurassic Park*?

Friend: My sister couldn't wait! She told everyone at work, all her friends in the neighborhood, and even the kids at the school where she teaches. Her husband told his fellow lawyers and they went to see the movie too.

You: So, all these people purchased tickets and bought some snacks. Then what happened?

Friend: I guess they told their friends about Jurassic Park. It's hard to keep a movie like this a secret. I mean, the dinosaurs looked real. They weren't some Godzilla-type puppets. The dinosaurs looked like the real thing.

You: Well, what you just **did** was network marketing. We do it every day. Network marketing is just **recommending** what we like to other people, usually our friends and acquaintances.

If what we recommend seems interesting to our friends, they might try it. Our friends are under **no obligation** to see *Jurassic Park*. They can take our recommendation or ignore it. That's strictly up to them.

We did our obligation, educating them that this choice was available. The decision to take advantage of this choice is up to them. That's called networking.

Friend: In that case, sure, I do networking every day. So what's the big deal about networking?

You: Most people do network marketing every day. They just don't get paid for it.

Let's take the movie theater example with *Jurassic Park*. The owner of the movie theater might have paid for some newspaper and radio advertising. However, these types of promotional advertising don't work very well. We're flooded with these commercial messages and ignore them. Plus, we don't trust these advertisements.

However, we do trust and respect our friends. When a friend tells us that a movie is great, we listen. That word-of-mouth recommendation from a friend is worth ten times the effect of a radio commercial.

When the movie owner tallies up his attendance for the month, he'll realize that most of the moviegoers came because of word-of-mouth recommendation.

So, in a sincere act of gratitude, the movie owner will send you a word-of-mouth advertising bonus check.

Why? Because if it wasn't for you, all those extra people would never have gone to his theater.

Friend: I'll never see that check in the mail. Movie theaters don't work that way. They keep the advertising savings from our word-of-mouth promoting, and let us work for free. So, how do we collect?

You: Some companies realize that word-of-mouth **recommending** and promoting is more powerful than any advertising budget. These companies market their products exclusively through word-of-mouth advertising.

They don't expect us to work for free, so these companies share their advertising budget with us by sending us a monthly bonus check for our efforts.

I feel that as long as we are doing the work anyway (recommending and promoting), we might as well collect a monthly check for our time and effort.

Friend: Are you sure everyone does network marketing every day?

You: Absolutely!

Have you ever recommended a restaurant to a friend? Your friend enjoys the meal and tells other acquaintances about the fine restaurant. The increase in food sales is appreciated by the restaurant.

You did the work.

You **recommended** and **promoted** the restaurant you liked. However, you **didn't** get paid for it. Most restaurants won't share their advertising budget. You do the promotional work for free.

Your **recommendation** was more effective than two-for-one dinner coupons, billboard advertising, and newspaper advertising. Networking is the most effective way to educate other prospects about goods and services.

Why? Because people listen and trust the opinions of people they personally know.

If you wanted a brain surgeon for an important operation, which method would you use?

Method #1: Would you check to see which surgeon had the biggest ad in the Yellow Pages? Would you listen to the surgeon with the snappiest ad jingle on the radio?

Method #2: Or, would you seek out someone you knew, a person who had an experience with a brain surgeon, and ask his opinion? Would you ask the opinion of a previous patient, or possibly your family physician?

I'm sure you'd use method #2. When it comes to brain surgery, you want an opinion you can trust.

Again, this is an example of networking. The friend or family physician freely offered his opinion and **recommended** a brain surgeon. You were under no obligation to use his **recommendation**, but at least you were educated about another possible option in your decision-making process.

Friend: Oh, I get it. Since I am recommending and promoting things every day, I might as well get paid for it, right?

So how do I collect?

***

Now your prospect no longer resists the idea of network marketing as being strange or unusual. Your prospect respects network marketing and he wants to know how he can collect a check for his efforts.

This conversation is easy. It doesn't threaten your prospect, and educates your prospect on how networking really works.

If your prospect is smart, he will quickly figure out that there are two types of people in the world:

1. Those people who do network marketing every day and get paid for it.

2. Those people who do network marketing every day and **don't** get paid for it. These people insist on doing network marketing for **free**, and that's okay. It makes the world a better place.

Everyone does network marketing every day!

Here are a few more examples:

- Recommending a school for the children.

- Recommending a web page.

- Recommending a pub with a great atmosphere.

- Recommending a favorite song or artist.

- Recommending a blind date.

- Recommending a brand of automobile.

- Recommending your favorite dish or recipe.

- Recommending a stock or an investment.

- Recommending an attorney or a tax accountant.

- Recommending a dentist.

- Recommending your favorite television show.

- Recommending a weight-loss secret.

- Recommending a great clothing store.

- Recommending a church.

- Recommending some new friends.

- Recommending computer software.

- Recommending a good book.

These are all examples of network marketing in action. You **recommend** the things and services that you like. The prospect is under no obligation to accept your recommendations.

Your only job is to educate and present additional choices or options for the prospect. Your job is not to make the decision for the prospect. That's the prospect's right and responsibility.

It is your responsibility to give the prospect an opportunity to learn this information.

However, you are not responsible for the decisions your prospects make after hearing this information.

Your prospect has many variables and situations in his life that he must balance along with your recommendations. Respect that.

The prospect will make a decision based upon what is happening in his life, so don't feel offended if a prospect uses a different dentist because his brother-in-law just graduated from dental college. Or, don't take it personally if the prospect doesn't go to the restaurant that you like. He may have completely different tastes in food.

Are You a Rock and Roll Star?

Did you write that musical hit that the world couldn't resist? And because of your musical talents, do you receive a music royalty check in the mail for thousands of dollars each month?

No? No musical talent? No skill at writing hit records?

Well, are you a famous novelist?

Are you interviewed on all the television talk shows? Do publishers bid record amounts of money for the rights to your next mystery novel? And, because of your captivating writing talent, do you receive thousands of dollars in royalties from your publisher every month?

Or, do you own a couple million dollars' worth of high-grade stocks and bonds? And, every month do you receive a dividend check for thousands of dollars, conveniently sent to you from your broker?

Or, did you arrange to be adopted by a rich family? And did that family leave you thousands of dollars in monthly inheritance income from their many trust funds?

Or, do you have to work for a living?

If you are like most people, you have to work for a living. If you don't work, you don't get paid.

What's different in the above examples? Well, if you were a successful rock star, novelist, rich investor, or lucky

heir, you would receive money every month even if you
didn't go to work. That's called residual income.

What's residual income?

It's a lot different than linear income, the kind most
people have. You see, linear income continues only as long
as you continue the work.

- If you are a surgeon, you get paid whenever you
  perform a surgery. If you don't perform a surgery,
  you don't get paid.

- If you are a construction worker, you get paid when
  you work. If you decide not to work for the next 12
  months, chances are your employer is not going to
  pay you.

- If you drive a bus, you get paid. If you quit driving
  buses, you don't get paid.

That's how **linear** income works. You receive income
when you work. When you stop working, the income stops
coming.

Residual income is different.

**The best way to describe residual income is that when
you do something right just one time, you get paid over
and over again for what you did.**

So, you wrote a hit song ten years ago. Every time it
plays on the radio somewhere in the world, you get a little
royalty. Even though you finished writing your song ten
years ago, every month you receive a royalty check from
people who play your tune. You did it right one time, and
now you collect every month.

When you wrote that hit novel five years ago, you finished your work. Now, you receive regular royalty checks from continuing sales of your book from your friendly publisher. You did it right one time, and now you collect every month.

You invested the few million dollars you had lying around in your checking account six years ago into high-grade stocks and bonds. Now, every month you look forward to your monthly dividend checks. You did it right one time, and now you collect every month.

You called every duke, queen, business magnate, and rich sports star twenty years ago and asked to be adopted. Finally, one accepted your proposition. Every month your inheritance check reminds you that the adoption letter campaign of twenty years ago really paid off.

You did it right one time, and now you collect every month.

Residual income sounds nice, doesn't it? Unfortunately, most people have trouble developing a residual income.

Why? We can't sing or write music. We don't have publishing contacts for our hit novel. We don't have a few million dollars sitting in our checking account, waiting to be invested. And, worst of all, we can't find any rich people in failing health ready to adopt us.

However, there is hope.

There is another way to develop residual income. There's a way to get monthly checks for thousands of dollars so that we can do the things we want in life, so that we can achieve our dreams. And best of all, almost anyone can develop this residual income.

Tens of thousands of people have already developed lifelong residual incomes through the power of network marketing. How?

They simply recommended the products and services that they liked to others. When others use these products and services, a small royalty is paid to the person who did the recommending.

Over time, this can accumulate and get larger and larger every month. For some people, their royalties from recommending exceed their full-time incomes.

Why not recommend something now, and collect royalties for years and years and years?

I Can't Find Any Good Prospects!

Your distributor approaches you and says, "I talked to all my relatives and they said no. I talked to all my friends and they said no. Could you please help me find some good prospects?"

Well, you want to say, "If your relatives and friends hated what you said, strangers aren't going to like it any better. That's not the problem. You have to change what you say."

But that would be pretty direct. So instead, we can tell a story. You might want to use this story so they understand it is not about finding good people, it is about what we say to the people we meet.

And how did I learn this lesson personally? Let me tell you the story.

It's Not My Fault.

When I first started, I had one year and ten months of total failure.

I invested in a workshop to change my "luck," and at the workshop they asked me this question:

"Big Al, why can't you recruit anybody?"

A good question. So I said, "Well, I'm living in Chicago right now. There's snow on the ground and it is winter. There is no place for people to park at the opportunity meetings. And come December, we won't even have opportunity meetings. Our product is a lot more expensive than the competition and people can't afford it now. They are losing their homes or worried about their jobs. The economy is pretty bad. People don't want to be a salesman. The meetings are too far away. The sponsor doesn't return my phone call and ..."

They interrupted, "Big Al, do other people in Chicago get bonus checks?"

I said, "Yeah. Some get huge bonus checks. I work ten times harder and I get nothing. That's not fair."

And then they dropped this bomb on me. "Big Al, the people in Chicago that get big bonus checks, do they have the same weather you do?"

Ouch.

"Same company?"

Ouch.

"Same product?"

Ouch.

"Same product pricing?"

This was really starting to hurt.

"Same territory?"

Groan.

"Same prospects?"

This was brutal.

Everything was exactly, one hundred percent, the same between the people who got huge bonus checks and me, who got nothing, except one thing.

When the people who got huge bonus checks talked to the very same people that I spoke to, they simply chose a different sequence of words. They simply changed the words they said, and everything changed.

Now, my mother didn't drop me on my head. I'm not stupid. I said, "I will stand around the people that make big bonus checks and listen to what they say and try their words."

60 days later, I had a full-time income just by changing the words I said.

***

This little story of what happened to me motivates the new distributor to stop looking for pre-sold prospects to ruin. Now the new distributor will eagerly learn "Ice Breakers" and other skills that use trained, tested words.

I let new distributors know that they can have moderately good success quickly in their career, by just learning trained, skilled, proven first sentences. They don't have to master everything immediately, but they do have to start their conversations with prospects right.

So how do I get them motivated to take the time to learn great first sentences? With a story, of course.

At a fast-start training for new distributors, here is the story I would use.

The Marriage Proposal.

How many people here have ever been married? Well, you know you have to have a successful proposal presentation ... or, you won't get married.

Let's say a young man wants to marry a young lady. He gets down on one knee, takes her hand between his hands, looks lovingly into her eyes, and as he stares into her eyes, his first sentence is this:

"If you marry me, every Tuesday night I will take you out for moonlight walks in the park, every Friday night we'll have candlelit dinners, and every Sunday night I will take out the garbage and be a good family man."

If the young lady likes the young man, she will probably say, "Yes."

Why? Because he had a great first sentence.

Now, will that young man make mistakes over the next 30, 40, 50 years? Absolutely. But because his first sentence was so good, she's going to forgive his mistakes for the rest of his life.

Now, let's do another proposal.

The young man gets down on one knee, takes her hand between his hands, looks lovingly into her eyes, and as he stares into her eyes, his first sentence is this:

"If you marry me, you get to keep the ring."

Ouch. Let me ask the ladies here. What are the odds of this marriage happening? Slim to none. (Some ladies might want to know the size of the ring before making this final decision.)

Most ladies would think, "Oh boy, what a cheap person. Do I really want to be married to somebody like this?"

And it is over.

No matter what this young man says after this first sentence, it's over. He can do a 3-D magic card trick, show slides of his childhood and it's not going to make any difference, because his first sentence was bad.

And that is exactly what happens when we talk to a prospect. If our first sentence is bad, our prospect is not going to be listening to us, won't be open-minded, won't hear the facts, and our prospect won't join.

***

It doesn't matter how fancy or impressive our presentation is, we are dead if our first sentence is bad.

Credibility Builds Trust.

Our prospects want what we have to offer, but many times we describe it poorly and the prospect rejects what we have described.

It is how you describe and tell your story that matters most. Prospects don't understand a business and all of its details before they start their new business. They simply understand the story you describe.

So ask yourself, "How good is the story I tell to prospects?"

And of course, that reminds me of a story ...

Too Good To Be True.

A network marketer dies and goes up to the pearly gates of heaven. Saint Peter meets him at the gates and says:

"Come on into my office and sit down, we have a new program here. Our new program is that you have a choice."

The man replies, "That sounds great. Tell me about it."

Saint Peter continues, "Well, in our new program you can go up into heaven, but if you prefer, you can go down into the other place."

The man paused for a second and said, "Well, I am the type of guy who likes to check things out. Would it be okay if I take a look at both places? I certainly wouldn't want to make a decision without all the facts."

Saint Peter agreed, took the man up to heaven, and showed him around for a little while.

"Hey, it's pretty nice up here," commented the man. "It is quiet, serene, and peaceful. But you know, I am quite an active guy, so would you mind if I took a look at the other place?"

"No problem," says Saint Peter. The two men went down to the "other place" and opened the door. The lights flashed, the music blared, people were drinking and dancing and having all kinds of fun.

"I just can't believe it. I never thought it would be like this! You know, I was kind of an old party guy back on earth. I really like this."

Saint Peter smiled and said, "Okay, let's go back into my office. It's time to make your decision."

The man went with Saint Peter to his office, sat down and said, "Well, heaven was really great. Nice and quiet, peaceful and serene. But you know, back on earth I really was a party animal. I never expected the 'other place' to be like that. Honestly, I am going to have to choose down below, the 'other place.'"

Saint Peter replied, "We accept your decision. Come on down."

They went down below, opened the door, but this time flames roared out. Saint Peter pushed the man inside and slammed the door shut. A big guy grabbed the man and yelled, "Here's a shovel. Start shoveling coal."

After twenty minutes of shoveling coal into the furnace, the man stopped and looked at himself. He was dirty, hot, and sweaty. He looked to the big guy who gave him the shovel and said, "I don't understand this at all. A while ago I came down here and there was music, drinking and dancing. It was so wonderful. What happened????"

The big guy turned to the man and said, "Ah, yes ... well, that was our opportunity meeting!"

***

Today's prospects are sophisticated. They are smart and can smell hype and exaggeration. If we oversell our opportunity, we lose credibility with our potential distributors. Our prospects come to an opportunity meeting to hear a fair evaluation of a business opportunity. They did not come to hear a one-sided pep rally that borders on a carnival atmosphere. And if we oversell at our opportunity meeting, our prospect will have unrealistically high expectations, and then quickly quit when these high expectations aren't met.

Place yourself in a prospect's shoes. How would you feel if the audience applauded the speaker's every phrase? You would feel that you were sitting in an infomercial. You wouldn't join because you felt you needed to hear the other side of the story.

Or what would happen if you did join? In a few days, reality would hit you squarely in the forehead. When you experienced the hard work it takes to achieve those fantastic incomes promised, you would feel deceived and resentful. Not a good attitude for success.

Can you avoid overselling and still get results? Yes! You may experience even better results if you practice a little **underselling** in your presentation. Then your prospect will mentally add more value to what you say.

Underselling builds credibility. Credibility builds trust. Isn't that what sponsoring is all about?

As a businessman, trust is more important than marketing. Why?

Even if your marketing message is great, if you don't have the trust of your prospects, they won't believe your great marketing message.

To get your new distributor to understand the value of creating trust, you can tell this short humorous story.

Building Trust.

A distributor passed away and went to heaven. Arriving at the pearly gates, Saint Peter said, "Come on in. I'll show you around. You'll like it here."

Walking through the gates, the distributor noticed clocks everywhere. There were grandfather clocks, wall clocks, watches, and clocks in every corner. It appeared that heaven was nothing more than a giant clock warehouse.

Surprised at how heaven looked, the distributor asked, "Saint Peter, what's the deal? Why are all these clocks here in heaven?"

Saint Peter replied, "The clocks keep track of things on earth. There is one clock for each person. Every time the person on earth tells a lie, his clock moves one minute."

"For instance, this clock is for Sam, the used car salesman. If you watch it closely, it will move."

"Click." The minute hand on Sam's clock moved one minute. "Click." It moved another minute. "Sam must be closing a customer right now," said Saint Peter. "The minute hand on his clock moves all day."

The distributor and Saint Peter continued walking. Soon, they came to a clock with cobwebs on the minute hand. "Whose clock is this?" asked the distributor.

"That clock belongs to the Widow Mary. She is one of the finest, God-fearing persons on earth. I bet her clock hasn't moved in a year or two."

They continued walking and touring heaven. The distributor enjoyed watching the clocks of all his friends. When the tour was finished, the distributor said, "I've seen everyone's clock except the clock that belongs to my worthless sponsor. Where is his clock?"

Saint Peter smiled, "Just look up. We use his clock for a ceiling fan."

***

How do your customers, prospects, and distributors perceive your new distributor's credibility? Is he known as an honest straight-shooter? Or, is he considered just a salesman who exaggerates facts to make a sale?

Trust is what builds a long-term business.

Thinking Like A Business Person, Not A Jobholder.

Your new distributors have jobs. They think like jobholders and try to run their new network marketing business ... like a job. They don't understand what it takes to run a business.

But maybe it would be better if I describe this with a story.

No Paycheck.

You get hired for a new job. To impress the boss you work hard every day. At the end of the month you come to the accounting department to pick up your paycheck, and they say, "I am sorry, no paycheck, you just started this month."

You think, "Hmmm, okay. They probably just pay a month in arrears." Then you continue to work hard another month on your job.

Now, at the end of the second month, you come for your paycheck and they say, "No, no paycheck for you this month."

How do you feel? What are you going to do?

Well, you already have this job, and it will take a long time to find another job, so you work hard again for one month. This time you come for your paycheck and they say, "Sorry, no paycheck."

What will you do now?

Quit!!!!

If you work on your job and they don't pay you, you quit. That's how it works.

***

Now, it is that type of thinking your new distributor brings into his network marketing business. Unless he is prepared by you, the sponsor, he will quit if he doesn't earn a bonus check quickly.

You have to teach the new distributor the difference between building a business that will pay off forever, and working a job that will only pay you for the hours worked.

Here is a simple story that shows why most businesses take time to build.

The Casino.

Let's say Donald Trump wants to build a casino in your hometown.

The first year is spent looking for a location and securing a building site. Next, Donald creates a public relations campaign about the casino and the jobs it will create so that the local residents will support the project instead of resisting the construction.

After the successful public relations campaign, Donald starts negotiating with the local government for permits, licenses, and building approvals. After twelve months of negotiations and hearings, the casino project is approved by the city council.

Bids are put out to contractors for the construction of the casino. After reviewing the bids, construction can start.

First, a giant hole is dug into the ground for the foundation of the mega-casino. Three months of digging creates a huge hole.

Donald comes by the next day to review his progress. He walks up to the big hole in the ground, looks down and says, "I quit. I have spent three years on this project and haven't earned a penny yet!"

Do you really think Donald would say that? Of course not. He is a successful businessman. He knows he has to build the casino first before he can start earning money.

So Donald finishes his casino project even though he hasn't earned a penny yet.

When the casino is finished, it is an enormous cash-generator. Money and profits pour in day after day after day for years and years and years.

That's business. Invest time, money, and energy now, and get a perpetual payoff later.

That is how our network marketing business works. We need to work hard now to gather customers and distributors, and then later we can enjoy the cash bonuses, month after month after month. We are business people now, not employees.

***

Most prospects are afraid of failing. Here is a story to let them know that it is okay to fail in business.

Start Failing Now.

A young man wanted to know the secret of success. His business had recently failed. His spouse, relatives, and in-laws pleaded with him to quit dreaming and get a good solid 9-to-5 job.

The young man made an appointment with the richest man in his city. "Please, please tell me the secret of your success. Is it a special talent? Is it knowledge? What made you successful?"

The rich man smiled. "Let me tell you a story."

"The first time I tried going into business for myself, I failed miserably. My second business failed before I even started. The third business I mismanaged. I thought that you needed a 50% success ratio to succeed. I was wrong."

The young man asked, "Do you mean you have to do better than a 50% success ratio?"

"No," continued the rich man, "you hardly ever have to be right. I failed in 19 consecutive businesses. On the average, I lost $1,000 per try, or a total of $19,000. On my twentieth attempt, I succeeded in my first business. The profits in the first year were over $100,000. So you see, I lost $19,000 on 19 mistakes, and made $100,000 on my first success. You can be wrong and fail 19 out of 20 times and still succeed!"

The young man smiled. "You don't have to be smart, knowledgeable, or talented to succeed. You just have to be persistent. You can be wrong 95% of the time and it still won't keep you from success."

***

Do you have distributors who quit at the first disappointment? Do your friends and relatives discourage you from trying again?

Have courage. Don't quit. You only have to have one success. When you are rich and famous, everyone forgets your 19 mistakes. Why? Your 19 mistakes won't matter as long as you continue to reach for your success.

If you never do anything, you won't make a mistake. Is that what you want for your life? Of course not. Get started now and make some mistakes so success will come your way.

It makes sense to have our new distributors attend training to learn how to think like a businessman. But what if they don't want to go to training? Then try this story.

The Lumberjack.

An experienced lumberjack walked past one of the new recruits. The new recruit viciously chopped away at the large tree but only managed to bruise the bark. Seeing the hard work and wasted effort, the experienced lumberjack said, "Hey, why don't you sharpen your ax? It will make you much more efficient."

The new recruit answered, "No. I can't take the time to sharpen my ax. I'm busy trying to cut down this tree."

***

Many new network marketing distributors suffer from the "dull ax" syndrome. They set goals, work hard, but never reach the success they desire. Why? Because they never took the time to sharpen their "ax" by learning new, effective skills. These distributors waste effort, waste resources, and waste their careers. They only need to take a little time away from their frenzied futility to learn the skills that would serve them for a lifetime.

As network marketing expert, Tom Paredes, says, "You need training even if you get a job at McDonald's flipping hamburgers. So why not expect to invest some time and effort in learning new skills for a career in network marketing?"

What happens when new distributors venture into network marketing uninformed? Let's go back to our new lumberjack.

The story continues ...

It seems the new lumberjack finally got tired of beating his dull ax against the tree. In desperation, he went into town to the local hardware store. The manager of the hardware store said, "Yep. Your ax sure is dull. But, if I were you, I wouldn't get the ax sharpened. There is a new way of cutting trees that is even better than a sharp ax. It's called a chainsaw."

"Just give me that chainsaw and I'm outta here," said the new lumberjack. He took the chainsaw and disappeared into the woods.

Two days later the new lumberjack returned to the hardware store. He was sweaty, had blisters on his hands, and looked very depressed. He found the store manager and said, "Hey, you. You sold me this chainsaw and promised me better results. I've been slaving away in the woods for two days and still haven't finished cutting down my first tree!"

The store manager replied, "Well son, just hand the chainsaw over here and let me see what the problem is." The store manager examined the chainsaw and saw nothing wrong. Then he grabbed the starter cord and gave it a big pull.

"B-b-b-b-r-r-r-r-r-r-o-o-o-o-o-o-o-o-o-o-m-m-m-m-m-m!" The chainsaw belched some smoke and began to run.

"Hey! What's that noise?" the new lumberjack exclaimed.

It seems that the new lumberjack never took the time to learn the features or even how to use his new tool.

***

The same is true in network marketing. One must not only acquire new tools, but also the knowledge on how to use them. And, in this rush, rush society, it will take some discipline and time investment to perfect one's new business-building skills.

The payoff? Almost anything you want. All you have to do is be willing to change. After all, Michelangelo changed from painting floors to painting ceilings when he got the Sistine Chapel job. The same new opportunities await you with your brand-new network marketing skills.

But what if your new distributor does just the opposite? What if your new distributor spends all of his time in training, and never goes out to start his business. Need a story that you can tell this distributor?

More Dangers of Overtraining.

A middle-aged man had worked as the school's janitor for 25 years. Today, the school superintendent called him into his office.

"I've looked at your original application from 25 years ago. It says here that you never went to college. Is that right?"

The janitor replied, "That's correct. I never attended college."

"Your application doesn't show that you graduated from high school. Did you attend high school?"

"No. I never attended high school."

"I'm sorry to tell you this, but the school board has a new policy. All school employees must have at least a high school diploma. For 25 years you have done a terrific job, but I have to let you go. Rules are rules."

The janitor turned in his mop and went home. "What can I do? I've been a janitor all my life. Maybe I can start my own janitorial business."

The first company he contacted said, "Sure, you can do the clean-up here. I remember how you did such a great job at the school."

The next company said the same thing. Soon the janitor had more buildings to clean than he could personally handle. He hired an assistant.

Business continued to grow. Soon the janitor hired more employees. His customers were so happy with his work that they gave him additional small construction contracts.

After a couple of years, the janitor became quite wealthy. He had dozens of employees, trucks, equipment, and a six-figure bank account.

Then, one day he received a letter to come down to his bank. The vice president greeted the janitor and said, "It's a pleasure to have you come down to our bank. We've never seen you here. Your employees always make your deposits. We checked our old records and found that you never signed the signature card to open your bank account. Could you sign it for us now, just to keep our records straight?"

The janitor replied, "I don't know how to write. You see, I've never been to school. Would an "X" be okay?"

"Sure. No problem." The banker didn't want to offend his largest customer. "This is amazing! Here you are, a janitor, who has succeeded in business and become our biggest account. Just think what you could have achieved with an education!"

"Heck!" said the janitor. "If I had an education, I'd still be a janitor!"

***

Sometimes action is better than any other solution.

And speaking of a business, will your new distributor set goals?

If he sets goals, will they be specific ... or just some vague generalities that represent hopes and wishes?

If you want your new distributor to set specific goals, here is a short story to impress the importance of being specific.

Goals Must Be Specific.

Once upon a time, a young lady visited an antique shop. While browsing, she noticed a beautiful mirror. When told that the price was $5,000, the young lady gasped. "How could this mirror, lovely as it is, be worth $5,000?"

The shop owner replied, "This is a magic mirror. Look into the mirror, make a wish, and your wish will come true."

Satisfied, the young lady took the magic mirror home and proudly showed her purchase to her husband.

"$5,000 for a mirror! You must be out of your mind!" screamed her husband. "Let's see a demonstration of your stupid mirror."

The young lady stepped in front of the mirror and said, "Mirror, mirror, on the wall. I wish for a beautiful, full-length mink coat." Instantly, a beautiful, full-length mink coat appeared on her shoulders. She turned to her husband, smirked, and left to show her neighbors the new coat.

The husband looked around and saw no one watching. He stepped in front of the mirror and said, "Mirror, mirror, on the wall. Make me irresistible to women!"

Instantly, the mirror turned the husband into a bottle of perfume.

***

When distributors complain about not making enough money right away, I tell them the story of what happened to me in Hawaii.

One Good Investment Is Worth a Lifetime of Labor.

While on the Norwegian Star cruise ship, I sat across the table from a very, very old man. He told me his life story in about one minute. This is what he said:

"I moved to California in 1939 and started a bank with a couple of friends. California grew, so our bank grew along with it. Eventually we became the fourth largest bank in California. A big bank bought us and we made millions of dollars on the sale.

"And young man, here is what I learned. That one good investment is worth a lifetime of labor."

And then I thought, "And if we don't have a good investment, then we are sentenced to a lifetime of labor!"

We all know someone who bought an inexpensive house on the coast and 30 years later sold it for a million dollars. Or, we know about someone who invested in Apple stock 20 years ago.

There are plenty of case studies of individuals who made one investment, and that investment earned them more money than they ever earned at their jobs.

Everyone wants to have a great investment, but here are the excuses I hear:

- "I don't have any money to invest in stocks."

- "I am afraid of taking the money out of our savings account as I might lose my investment."

- "Real estate is too expensive now. I can't afford to buy property."

- "I don't know what investment to make. I have never done this before and I am afraid of taking a risk."

Well, these excuses work. People don't even try to get one good investment.

But we can change that. With network marketing, all people really have to invest is time into their businesses. And if they are serious, they can afford to invest a little time.

That means little or no financial risk.

Now there are no excuses for not having an investment that could pay off big.

***

Just think of this. Maybe your distributors complain that they just haven't made any money yet. Could be true. But, there is a chance that they may find one good person who will earn them $1,000 a month, every month for the rest of their lives.

Now, that's a great investment, right?

Try to use this principle to keep your distributors "in the game." After all, if they quit, there is no chance that their investment will ever pay off.

And what if your new distributor was shy? Could your new distributor tell this "cruise story" once a day? The story only takes a minute, and it is only a story. No rejection.

Your new distributor could say, "Want to hear a quick story about what happened on a cruise ship?"

Most prospects would say, "Yes."

Now, if your new distributor invested one minute a day telling this story (it could be done on coffee break), and did this for one month, 30 prospects would have heard that story.

Out of 30 prospects, some might say, "Hey, you're right. I need a good investment." Let's say only 10% said that. That would mean sponsoring three new distributors a month, just with this story.

And the 27 people who heard the story and just didn't see how it would change their life? Maybe they were having a "bad coffee day." They would say, "Nice story." And life would go on.

Three new distributors sponsored a month. One little story. Is that better than your distributors are doing now?

And while we are on the subject of how to find good distributors who take action:

"Blue" personalities are natural born storytellers. They tell stories all day long. And because they like to talk, some of their stories go on and on and on.

These "blue" personalities love meeting new people and will talk to anyone, anywhere.

To locate a "blue" personality, simply say this to any cold prospect or someone willing to give you referrals:

"Who do you know that is a good storyteller?"

It is easy for someone to give a referral to a good storyteller. No salesmanship needed here.

When you get to the "blue" personality, the natural-born storyteller, say this:

"There are two types of people in the world. Those who tell stories, and those who get paid for telling stories."

Then, shut up. The rest is up to the prospect. The "blue" personality either "gets it" or doesn't. It is just that simple.

Now remember, "blue" personalities are great at meeting new people, but terrible at follow-up. You will have to help out there.

The Notification Principle.

The first priority of new distributors is to avoid rejection. But what do we do as sponsors?

We tell them to make a list, call all of their friends, and get beat up, humiliated, and embarrassed.

Why does this happen?

Because our new distributor doesn't yet know exactly what to say and exactly what to do. Our new distributor hasn't had time to begin learning the skills needed in his network marketing business. So of course the relatives and friends will hear an invitation from a nervous, untrained, and uncertain new distributor. That's a recipe for disaster.

Our new distributor will try to sell, force, manipulate and entice their contacts into coming to a meeting, joining the business, buying some product. And when you try to sell anything, there is a huge risk of someone telling you "No."

Let's see what happens in the real world.

You're ecstatic! Your brand-new distributor has signed the paperwork, mailed it to the company, and is now waiting for his new distributor kit and products to arrive.

As a well-trained sponsor, you've organized a "Getting Started" training within the first 48 hours of your new distributor's network marketing career.

You sit down at the kitchen table with your new distributor, pull out your Getting Started manual and immediately turn to the "Memory Jogger" section and start reading:

- Who do you know with red hair?

- Who do you know that drives a mini-van?

- Who does your taxes? Your hair? Your lawn? Your car repairs?

- Do you have your college directory handy?

- Do you have a copy of your family tree?

- How about your pre-school yearbook?

You keep going on and on, asking more questions to jog your new distributor's memory.

You take a moment between reading questions to breathe, look across the table at your new distributor's list and -- **there are only 8 names on it**! There should be at least 50 names by now! You look up to see fear and doubt on your distributor's face as he shrugs and says,

"I really don't know anybody else."

Out of frustration you ask a few more questions from your memory jogger ... but still, your new distributor comes up empty, no more names.

Did you sponsor a "dud?"

We lip-sync through this uncomfortable exercise, yet we rarely take a moment to see if it actually works or not. Why not, for a moment, consider what is going through your new distributor's mind? You may be surprised.

Your distributor could be thinking:

"I don't want to talk to anybody about this business until I make my first bonus check."

Or,

"I'm not comfortable having my sponsor talking to my friends about the business. What if my sponsor high-pressures or embarrasses my friends?"

Or,

"The more names I put down, the more rejection I might have to face."

Most distributors are not duds and are not lazy. However, **they will avoid anything that involves rejection.**

Why not turn the exercise into something that your distributor **wants to do**?

What if you told your new distributor:

"You don't have to ask anyone on your list to join your network marketing business or even ask them to buy product."

Now that sounds a lot safer to your new distributor. Most of your new distributor's fears are starting to melt away.

Not asking people to join your business is **rejection-free**.

Or maybe you have a new distributor, who says,

"Oh, I don't want to talk to my friends and relatives. They wouldn't understand. I couldn't convince them to join my program. Instead, let me talk to **total strangers** from another country. Maybe I'll just try to sell them over the phone or over the Internet. Where can I run an ad, buy some leads, or mail some prospecting postcards?"

If friends and close contacts don't like your presentation, strangers will like your presentation even less.

If we can't enroll people we know, people with whom we already have some sort of positive relationship, what makes us think that we can enroll total strangers?

Maybe we just think things will change if we find new people who don't know us.

Let's face it. When we decide to talk to strangers instead of our warm market of contacts, we're saying to ourselves:

"I don't believe in me."

"I don't believe in my opportunity."

"I don't believe in my product."

"I'm too ashamed to talk to my friends."

"I don't think this opportunity is a good deal for others."

"I'm worried about what my friends will think of me."

"I'm afraid that my friends will not join and that I'll feel rejected."

"What if my program fails? I better make certain that I only sign up strangers who don't know me."

"What if I fail? I wouldn't want my friends and family to know that I even tried."

And if we **decide** to keep our opportunity a secret from our friends and family, is that fair to them?

No.

So even before we read our distributor kit, before we start improving our presentation, before we start working on self-image, before asking our sponsor about mailing lists or ads, before anything else, we must first fulfill our one and only obligation in network marketing.

And what is that obligation?

We must notify our friends, relatives, neighbors and co-workers that we have decided to start our own part-time network marketing business.

Right now **our first obligation** is simply to let them know that we have started our own business.

Our job is **not** to sell our products or to convince our prospects to join.

Later we will **educate** our prospects with the facts so that they can make the best choice for themselves.

That's it.

Network marketing is not high-pressure selling, convincing, manipulating, cold-calling, or a coercing business. Networking is simply giving prospects an additional choice in their lives, and allowing them to accept that choice if it helps them get what they want.

That's our job – educating our prospects. That's what we do as networkers.

Great news for beginning network marketers.

As we've seen, network marketing isn't so complicated after all. Our full-time job is educating prospects and letting them make their own decisions.

However, we do have one very serious obligation as network marketers. When we sponsor a new distributor we should say something like this:

"You are not obligated to make lots of retail sales. Sure it would be nice, but it's not mandatory."

"You are not obligated to buy lots of products and services. Again, that would be nice, but you are not obligated to do so."

"You are not obligated to harass your friends to come to opportunity meetings."

"You are not obligated to go the company convention."

"You are not obligated to give recruiting presentations every night of the week."

"You are not even obligated to return my phone calls!"

Wow! Now your new distributor is excited. The pressure is gone. He doesn't have to make phone calls asking his relatives and friends to buy products or join.

Your new distributor is thinking:

"Now this is a great opportunity. I'm not obligated to do any of those things. But wait, he said there was an obligation. Just one obligation. So what is that obligation?"

Yes, we only have a **single** obligation to fulfill. Everything else in network marketing is optional. What is that obligation in our business?

We must notify our friends, relatives, neighbors and co-workers that we have decided to start our own part-time network marketing business.

That's it. There's nothing more to our obligation.

You see:

- We don't have to sell our friends on our products or services.

- We don't have to sponsor our neighbors into our network marketing business.

- We don't have to invite our co-workers to opportunity meetings.

- We don't even have to explain our business or products if our relatives don't ask us for more information.

Our only obligation is to **notify** our friends, relatives, neighbors and co-workers that we have decided to start our own part-time network marketing business.

You mean we don't have to learn fancy presentations or constantly try to show our program to unwilling relatives?

Yes! Exactly.

We don't have to give presentations to our contacts unless they specifically **ask** us for such a presentation.

We don't have to push or sell products to the unwilling.

And, we don't need to make intrusive sales pitches during funerals, wedding receptions or family reunions.

Uplifting, isn't it? It's nice to get that burden off our shoulders.

So why is **notifying** our contacts that we have started our own networking business so important?

Because we never want them to tell us,

"You never told me about your business."

If we simply announce that we are in network marketing, many of our contacts will nod their heads and say,

"That's nice."

And that's okay.

If they were interested, they could ask us for more information or attend an opportunity meeting. But, if they are not interested, we can go on with our lives, knowing that they were given a chance to get the full story, just by asking us for it.

Some of our contacts will say,

"Hey, I'm not excited about my job either. I want a little more time with my family too. So tell me a little bit about this networking business, would you?"

And that's okay too.

We can then give them as much information as they desire.

If you don't fulfill your obligation to notify your personal contacts … **terrible things** could happen. I use the following story so new distributors always remember to notify everyone they know.

How to Protect Yourself From a Machete-Wielding Neighbor.

Imagine that you have been a part-time network marketer for the past six months. You've saved every word-of-mouth advertising bonus check and now have enough money to take that dream vacation to Tahiti.

Your regular job paid your monthly expenses, so you were able to save all of those extra monthly bonus checks.

You go to your local airport, and as you enter the Air Tahiti 747 airplane, you think,

"It was a great decision to do a little network marketing on the side. If my business continues to improve, I'll be taking one of these nice vacations every three months! Thank goodness my sponsor told me about this network marketing opportunity."

When you arrive in Tahiti, you're taken to a glamorous beach. Gentle ocean waves help you relax in your hammock while the resort's staff delivers your favorite tropical beverage. The music is soothing. The wind is refreshing. And you can smell the barbecue teriyaki chicken on the grill just a few feet away.

Aaaahh! It doesn't get any better than this.

But wait!

You spot a small dot on the horizon, and it appears to be moving. Yes, it's definitely moving. The dot continues to grow. It's moving towards you.

After watching the dot grow larger and larger, you realize that the dot is actually a person. And, this person is dragging an old blanket behind him.

Soon that person walks right up to your hammock, spreads his old blanket on the sand, and plops down to catch some sun. You look down at the person on the blanket and suddenly realize that this person is your ...

Next door neighbor!

What a surprise! What a coincidence! You turn to your next door neighbor and say,

"Hi."

Your surprised neighbor stutters:

"Uh, uh, uh, it's you. I can't believe this! Here we are, thousands of miles away from home and it's you right here next to me! This is incredible!"

You answer,

"I'm quite surprised too. How come you're here enjoying a nice holiday?"

Your next door neighbor's face droops. His brow wrinkles and he sadly mumbles,

"Well, you know I live a miserable life. I have to keep three jobs going just to pay the rent for our family. I'm in debt up to my ears. My car loan is overdue. There is no chance to advance in my job. I don't have a penny to my name. I'm doomed!

"So I thought I might as well take a three-day holiday just once in my miserable life, in order to have that single pleasant memory before I die. And to get here, I took out another loan, I maxed out all five of my credit cards, I stole the money in my kids' college savings account, and I even broke into their piggy banks, just to scrape together enough money for this ticket.

"And what about you? How come you're here?"

Now comes the moment of truth.

You say,

"I got started in my own part-time networking business about six months ago. It's really great. I get paid for just letting people know about it. So, I saved up the last few bonus checks and here I am. This part-time business is so good, I'm thinking about taking another week's holiday here in three months. I tell you, this business is more than great! It's awesome. In fact, it's so wonderful that I ... uh, uh ... uh, I forgot to tell you about this, didn't I?"

Your neighbor's face turns red. Slowly he gets up from his blanket and walks to the ice carving by the teriyaki chicken grill. He grabs the razor-sharp machete and slowly starts walking towards you. As he draws back his arm ...

***

Whoops. Better stop here before it gets ugly.

As you see, if you don't fulfill your obligation to notify your personal contacts ... **terrible things** could happen.

Remember, we must give our personal contacts the opportunity to ask us for more information. We don't have to force our presentation on them. We don't have to sell them products. We don't have to high-pressure them to become distributors.

All we have to do is give them additional information if they ask for it.

This way your relatives and friends can never come back to you and say:

"You never told me about your opportunity."

That would be sad.

And that's how you avoid random machete attacks.

But if that story doesn't work for you, try this story.

How Not To Get Embarrassed
By Your Own Aunt.

Imagine that you are at your cousin's wedding. That evening, at the reception, you find yourself sitting at one of the dinner tables with about twelve other guests.

You notice your aunt, who at this point has had a bit too much free champagne, sitting at the same table. She's dominating the conversation and to your surprise one of the first things out of her mouth as she sits down is:

"I just joined this great home-based business last month called 'Opportunities Are Us' and I'm doing great!"

You can't believe it, you joined "Opportunities Are Us" over a year ago and never once asked your aunt to join or even let her know that you got involved!

But it gets worse. She then proceeds to go around the table asking each person if they have heard of "Opportunities Are Us." She's prospecting your warm market.

You begin to sweat. You are angry that she could have been in your group, but you did not notify her when you got involved.

And now it gets even worse! What are you going to say when she asks you if you've heard of "Opportunities Are Us?"

Are you going to say,

"Yes, I have heard of "Opportunities Are Us," and actually I joined over a year ago. But it's like this, well, because you're such a loser I didn't think you could ever do the business so I never let you know about it."

You wish you could just crawl underneath the table. This is going to be embarrassing.

The bad news continues.

Three months later you are at your company's national convention. With each passing hour you get more and more excited about all the new announcements. The distributor recognition event begins. The higher the pin level, the more admiration you feel for those walking across the stage.

All of sudden you hear your aunt's name over the convention sound system. Could it be your aunt? Nah, must be someone else with the same name. You look up on stage and ... and **it is your aunt**, in all her glory, walking across the stage to accept her new Triple-Platinum Star-Trek Commander Executive Pin. As you stare at her in awe, you notice her wink directly at you!

Life's not fair!

Talk about a nightmare!

You have been in the business a year longer, yet she's the one on stage, five pin levels higher than you!

You have been to more network marketing training events, you have been the host at your local opportunity meeting more often, you have read more books about this business, you know the compensation plan better, you have handed out more brochures, done more cold calls and even placed a national ad!

Your frustration kicks into overdrive.

"Why is my aunt on stage while I am sitting way in the back of the auditorium in the nosebleed section - struggling just to get to the next pin level?"

And for the next hour, you quietly daydream and make up dozens of different reasons justifying to yourself **why she's on stage and you're not.**

"She got lucky and probably signed up 3 leaders in her first month!"

"She has more time to build her business."

"She must have a better sponsor than I do."

"It must be easier to build the business once you are at the higher pin levels."

"The people at the corporate office like her better than me."

"She is more outgoing than I am."

"It's okay if it takes me 10 years longer than my aunt to get to the top, after all I am at least 10 years younger so I will get even."

"She has a better house for home meetings and a better television to show the company DVD on."

"She knows more people because she is older and lives in the city."

The bottom line is that she notified everyone in her warm market and you didn't.

Your aunt also makes sure every leader in her group goes through the notification process.

No matter what else you do in your business, if you aren't using notification, odds are that your business isn't growing as fast as you'd like it to be.

***

So don't you think it is a little bit unfair not to tell your personal contacts about this great business?

How would you feel if someone kept your network marketing company a secret from you?

Or, how would you feel if your neighbor quit his job, took family holidays every two months, and never told you about his secret good fortune, while you slaved away at a job you hated?

Give your personal contacts the opportunity to say,

"No, I'm not interested."

It will prevent serious machete wounds that could ruin your next holiday. Plus it will prevent embarrassing situations at your cousin's wedding reception.

Notify – not sell.

Whew! That's a long explanation of why we should notify everyone about our business. But let's look at notification in another way.

The Shoe Store.

Let's imagine you opened a shoe store in the local shopping mall. Wouldn't you notify everyone you know that you had opened your own shoe store?

Of course you would.

You wouldn't pressure them to come and buy shoes that day. You wouldn't take some boxes of shoes with you to sell at the family reunion, and you wouldn't be passing out shoe samples at funeral receptions, would you?

You would simply notify everyone you know that you had opened your own shoe store. Then, when the time was **right** for them to purchase shoes, they would contact you.

You see, everyone needs shoes, but they don't all need shoes today. For most people, when the time is right, they will think of you and your business, **if they know** you have a business.

Not everyone is ready to start their own part-time business today. Maybe tomorrow. Maybe next year. But for most of your contacts, today is not the day.

***

Or look at it this way.

If your daughter was getting married, would you notify everybody you know about the wedding? Of course you would.

You wouldn't invite them to an opportunity meeting to tell them about the upcoming wedding. You would just notify them about the wedding.

Out of every 100 people in your warm market **right now**, several are seriously looking for an additional way to make an extra paycheck every month. However, in most cases you never get these people to raise their hands, letting you know they are hot prospects!

Why?

Because you only contacted the first four or five people on your list, and then never notified the rest. You stopped!

Maybe you got rejected, discouraged, or distracted. It doesn't matter.

What happened is that many of your best contacts don't know you have a business.

So when you sit down and ask your new distributor to write down the names of everyone in their warm market, **share the notification principle with him first**.

Take the time to slowly explain exactly how notification can work for him. Tell your new distributor a story.

Share with him what could happen if he doesn't notify everyone in his warm market.

That way, instead of having him leaning backwards and fighting you every step of the way, he will lean forward and enthusiastically write down the name of everyone he knows!

You can make it a lot easier for your new distributors when you share with them the principle of notification.

The Principle of Reaction.

People go through life just **reacting** to events. They are like ping pong balls.

If the weather is good they are happy, if the weather is bad, they are sad. If their team wins, they are happy. If their team loses, they are sad. If they win the lottery, they celebrate. If they lose the lottery, they drink beer and moan about how life is treating them badly. If their spouse is happy, they are happy. If their spouse is sad, they are sad.

Do you realize that people are almost 100% reactive? All they can do is go through their entire life **reacting** to circumstances and people.

So do people join your business ... or join you? If people are **reactive**, that means they simply **react to you**, not your business.

This is an important principle for new distributors. They don't realize that prospects refuse great opportunities because they are reacting to the presenter.

Let's use some short stories and examples to help our new distributors realize that they are the source of their successes or failures.

The Ex-Spouse.

Imagine for a moment that you have an ex-spouse and your relationship with your ex-spouse is really, really bad.

Every time you get together it's nothing but fireworks, yelling and screaming.

However, your ex-spouse also has a fiancé. Every time your ex-spouse is with the fiancé, what happens? Kiss, kiss, smile smile.

But isn't the ex-spouse the exact same person?

Two completely different reactions and behavior because the ex-spouse is reacting to two completely different people.

***

So think about this. Prospects are neutral ... until they meet you.

They become good prospects or they become bad prospects by reacting to you, what you say and what you do.

Does that mean that we don't find good prospects and that we actually create them? Does that mean that we can actually create prospects-on-demand whenever we need them? We don't have to go out and look for hot prospects anymore?

Yes.

Finding good prospects is meaningless if we only turn them into bad prospects with what we say and what we do.

Now, new distributors don't want to take personal responsibility for their actions, so they will need a bit more proof. Here is another story to help.

Coffee Break.

Your boss asks you to get him a cup of coffee from the cafeteria upstairs. You step into the elevator and a stranger is already in the elevator.

So, the stranger is looking at you, and you're looking at the stranger, and here's what you do. You give that stranger the biggest, broadest smile that you can.

And if you do a great big smile like that, what is the stranger's normal reaction?

He smiles.

People are reactive. That stranger smiled because you smiled at him.

Need more proof?

So you go upstairs, you get a cup of coffee, a nice steaming hot cup of coffee for your boss. You jump on the elevator to go down to your office, and again, another stranger is already in the elevator.

You look at the stranger, you look down at your cup of hot coffee, and you do this:

WHOOOSH!

You throw the hot coffee on the stranger.

Will the stranger **react**?

Oh yes. In fact the stranger might react pretty violently. The stranger will question your family ancestry, question your IQ, and maybe say some words that won't be found in the dictionary. That stranger will jump up and down and will be very, very upset.

The stranger will **react**.

Now, did the stranger have to react? No. The stranger could have used his free will and said, "Those coffee stains look great next to my spaghetti stains. Thank you very much. And I was feeling kind of a chill and now my burning skin so warms me up."

Now, that is possible, but not likely.

People don't use their free will, they simply **react** to what you say and do.

Need more proof that people's actions depend on what you say and do?

Lunch.

Time for lunch. One restaurant in town. There is a line of 50 people waiting to place an order. Unfortunately, you are number 50 in this line.

Everyone with you at the back of this long line is depressed. They are saying, "This is terrible. This will take forever. The service here is so slow. I am so hungry. Couldn't they hire more staff?"

You want to test this principle of reaction, so you do this.

You just leave the line, walk all the way to the front of the line. You grab the food tray of the person who just got his food, stomp on his foot, take his tray, and walk away.

Now, is that person going to **react**? Absolutely.

He will be very upset.

Now, you take this tray of food, go all the way to that sad person near the back of the line, and you give it to the sad person and say, "I know it is a long line, here is some food, go ahead and sit down, enjoy yourself, and don't worry. It has already been paid for."

Will that person **react**? Yes. He will probably smile and **react** positively to you.

You have the power to control how people **react** to you. Why? Because you know the secret principle of **reaction**.

So if everyone you talk to is negative and refuses to join your business ... do you have to change other people?

No. It is impossible to change other people, isn't it?

However, you can change what you say and do and people will **react** differently.

If you are not getting the results you want, all you have to do is change your activity.

***

Need a good story to illustrate how this affects our sponsoring success? Want to see how people are attracted to you, not your business?

The Drunk.

You are walking in a rough neighborhood in a big city. It is late at night and you probably shouldn't be walking there alone.

As you are walking down the sidewalk, you see a drunk lying in the gutter. He is snoring loudly, holding a half-empty bottle of wine, and you realize he has been sleeping for quite a while because the spiders have built a cobweb between his nose and the curb. Flies are starting to circle around him, and this drunk is starting to smell.

So what happens? When you pass the drunk you try to avoid him by walking on the far edge of the sidewalk. But, just as you pass the drunk, the drunk reaches into his vest pocket and swoosh! He pulls out a brochure for his network marketing company and gives it to you.

You grab that brochure between your thumb and forefinger, hold it away from your body until you get to the very next trash bin, drop the brochure in the trash bin, just hoping, hoping, hoping that you don't pick up some dreaded disease.

So you keep on walking and up ahead is this giant of a person, leaning against the wall with his arms folded. You walk a little bit closer and you say, "That person is over seven feet tall and more than 300 pounds."

As you get a little closer you say, "That looks like Shaq O'Neal, the retired NBA All-Star center. It has to be him, because he is bouncing a basketball."

When you get near enough to see his jersey it says, "Shaq O'Neal."

You wonder, "What is he doing in this neighborhood at night? Did he lose his shoe endorsement contract? Or maybe he is waiting for his limousine?"

As you walk past Shaq O'Neal, he reaches into his vest pocket and whoosh! He gives you a brochure for his network marketing opportunity.

Now, would you look at his brochure? Sure.

The interesting thing to realize is that both Shaq O'Neal and the drunk in the gutter both represented the same network marketing business. In one case, you looked at the brochure, and in the other case, you didn't even look. Same company. Same opportunity. What was different? The person who gave it to you.

***

So, are people attracted to businesses or are they attracted to people?

People are attracted to people. They **react** to who you are, what you know, how you act, and what you say. You determine the behavior of your prospects. That is why we need to accumulate skills.

So instead of trying to change prospects, simply change what you say and do, and your prospects will react differently.

A Story For Ponzi, Pyramid, And Get-Rich-Quick Schemes.

Shock!

My worthless sponsor opened his mail and pulled out a cashier's check for $1,000,000.

He quickly cashed the check and deposited the $1,000,000 in his savings account. Life was going to be good.

On the way home from the bank, he quickly telephoned and:

1. Hired a personal assistant.

2. Ordered his Ferrari.

3. Hired a maid.

4. Bought a six-pack of premium beer.

After a good night's sleep, my worthless sponsor woke up to start enjoying his new lifestyle of a millionaire.

He called his personal assistant. No answer.

He looked in his driveway, and no Ferrari had been delivered.

The maid hadn't showed up for work.

"What's wrong with the world?!" he cursed.

So my worthless sponsor got into his old car, and drove into the city to fire some people and get the world to bow to his wishes. After all, he was a millionaire.

On the way to the city, John listened to the news on his radio. The newscaster reported:

"This will be my last broadcast. Yesterday ... everyone, including me, won $1,000,000."

***

Now, that story never happened.

Why?

Because there is no such thing as "easy money."

It there was secret formulas and "easy money" systems that worked, everyone would be a millionaire. Look around you. Are all of your friends, relatives and neighbors millionaires? No, they are still working on their jobs.

Yet, every day new people are seduced by schemes that sound like this:

> "No effort needed. We do all the work for you. Get rich fast. My secret formula is only available for 19 more days. Act fast. I'm sharing my million-dollar formula for only $19.95 because I want to donate to helping all the lazy people in the world who don't believe in giving value for money. And I was broke, born of orphan parents, raised by wolves, can't read, but this formula was given to me in a drug-induced dream. And I have testimonials from A.B. in Alabama and from C.D. in Florida. And if you can click a mouse, you can do this as millions of people on the Internet are waiting to send you money ..."

The lesson? We have to **learn** how to deliver **value** to prospects.

No one is going to give us $1,000,000 just for joining some Internet program. And no one will give us $1,000,000 if we sign up into the latest and greatest and hottest ground floor opportunity.

We have to deliver $1,000,000 in product, service and value. That's why people will give us $1,000,000.

You see, in life we have to ...

Pay Our Dues.

Imagine this.

There are two people, John and Mary.

John becomes a network marketer. He is lazy, doesn't get on conference calls, doesn't call his sponsor, doesn't learn new skills, avoids talking to prospects, and seldom gives out a sample.

His "hands-on" knowledge of talking with prospects is zero.

John simply sits around and waits for that lucky break ... and it comes!

The perfect prospect with the perfect connections with the perfect timing appears. Excellent!

And what happens to John's business?

Nothing.

John says the wrong things. His inexperience made him look nervous. And his prospect made a decision not to join.

Mary becomes a network marketer. She gets on every conference call she can, calls her sponsor regularly, learns new skills, gives presentations to "live" prospects, and passes out samples.

She learns how to talk with prospects. She accumulates experience.

While Mary is learning, struggling and interacting with prospects, that perfect prospect appears!

The perfect prospect with the perfect connections with the perfect timing is right in front of Mary. Excellent!

And what happens to Mary's business?

It explodes.

Why?

Because Mary had experience. She was more confident because she interacted with prospects daily. Each time she passed out a sample or a brochure, she learned a little bit more about dealing with people.

So when the perfect prospect appeared, Mary knew how to handle the presentation.

***

That's why we pass out samples, CDs, brochures, etc. We need to learn how to interact with prospects in real life.

The moral of this story is ...

We have to pay our dues!

Why Distributors Should Take Advice From Their Sponsors.

Bloody Tale of Vicious, Senseless Animal Slayings Guides Network Marketers to True Wisdom.

A donkey, a lion, and a fox decided to go out hunting for rabbits. After a pretty good day of hunting, they had collected a large pile of rabbits.

The lion says to Mr. Donkey,

"I would like you to divide the rabbits fairly among the three of us."

So, the donkey took the rabbits and made them into three equal piles and said,

"How is that?"

The lion immediately pounced on the donkey and killed him.

Then the lion threw all the rabbits on top of the donkey and made one big pile. The lion turned to Mr. Fox and said,

"I would like you to divide the rabbits evenly between the two of us."

The fox walked over to the pile of rabbits and took one little scrawny rabbit for himself and put it in his pile. He left the rest of the rabbits in a large pile and said,

"That pile of rabbits is for you, Mr. Lion."

The lion said,

"Mr. Fox, where did you learn to divide so evenly?"

And the fox replied,

"The donkey taught me."

***

The lesson in this story is that if you **only** learn from **your own** mistakes, then you might not live to the next mistake. ☺

However, if you can learn from other's mistakes, then you are wise.

Skills, But No Motivation.

So you sponsored that high-powered bank vice president. He has people skills, selling skills, and knows everyone in the city.

The only problem is, he hasn't contacted anyone. He has the tools and skills, but not the motivation to build. An easy way to understand this situation is with a story.

The Pile of Dirt.

If you understand how a pile of dirt can change your life, then you will understand what it takes to be successful in this business.

A lot of people think that skills, training and having lots of contacts is how you become successful in this business, but it takes something even more important.

Imagine a large pile of dirt about six stories high behind your house. It's a massive pile of dirt, and I am going to train you to become a professional dirt mover.

The first thing I am going to do is train you on the bulldozer. I will show you how to use the controls, move the levers and the blade up and down, how to move the dirt. I compliment you on how skilled you have become in controlling and working with the bulldozer.

The next day I am going to train you on a JCB earth mover and we are going to make the front shovel go up and down and the back shovel move around. You are exceptionally gifted on the JCB earth mover and have worked hard.

The following day I am going to teach you the theory and history of hand shovels and spades. This will help you know the history of how they were invented and how the cavemen used the original shovel. You will be well-grounded in the principles of moving dirt.

On the fourth day I am going to ask you to start applying the skills you have been taught and move a pile of dirt.

Unfortunately on your first day of work, you go outside to use the bulldozer and find it is out of fuel. You say, "Well, the fuel station is miles away, so forget it. I won't use the bulldozer."

You then walk over to the JCB earth mover and the front shovel is missing. You discover that the new front shovel is on backorder and hasn't been delivered yet. You decide you won't use that either.

Then it starts to rain. Your hair is getting stuck against your head. Your clothes are getting cold and wet. The mud is sticking to your feet. You see some of your friends walking by and since you now look terrible, you hide.

You say, "Well, I could probably move a bit of this mud with my hands if I have to, but I do not have any gloves on and I will probably get blisters or maybe even splinters. I am going to go inside, dry off, watch television and call it a day."

The pile of dirt and mud remains behind your house.

However, let us look at it again, and maybe this could have happened instead.

I ask you to go outside and move the pile of dirt behind your home. While looking at the dirt, you notice your baby daughter has climbed to the top of the pile of dirt and is playing. Suddenly your baby daughter starts to slide down the pile of dirt. The dirt is collapsing around your baby. Your baby is starting to be covered by the dirt.

Now what would you do?

Quickly you jump on the bulldozer to move the dirt to save your baby daughter, but the bulldozer is out of fuel. Would you say, "Well, it is a long way to get fuel. I tried my best."

No!

Without a thought, you would jump straight onto the JCB earth mover. The JCB earth mover has the front shovel missing, because it is on backorder. What would you do? Give up?

No!

You would say, "Well, the front shovel is missing but I certainly can use the back shovel."

And if the back shovel wasn't working, you would grab a hand shovel or a spade. Even if the rain started, you wouldn't mind. You would be there with your bare hands, digging away the dirt and mud because you needed to save your baby daughter.

You would do whatever it takes, you are motivated, and even if you didn't have any training, you would get the dirt moved because you have a **desire** and a **vision** and a reason to do it.

***

Yes, a desire, a vision, and a reason can be more important than knowledge.

You have to know what you want.

It could be you want more time with your family, or maybe you never want to leave your children at day care again. You might want some quality family time so you can take a cruise with them or a trip somewhere special.

We all know that our children will never really remember all the shoes and clothes we have bought for them, but they will always remember that special family holiday or time together.

It could be that you hate your job. Maybe you feel there is more to life than moving paper from one side of the desk to the other side of the desk. Maybe you want more in life than endless, mind-numbing hours commuting in traffic.

Maybe you have a dream that you can change your lifestyle and that you want to help others do the same. Or maybe you just want to take a nice Mediterranean or Caribbean cruise every month.

Your knowledge and skills are important, but you won't be motivated to use them unless you have a desire, a vision, and a reason to do this business.

And if you don't have the knowledge and skills to do this business, well, having that desire, that vision, and that reason to do the business will motivate you to seek out and master the knowledge and skills you need.

Or maybe just the thrill of being one's own boss, of controlling one's own life, is enough to motivate distributors to action. Here is a short story that is very non-threatening:

Why Bosses Don't Have to Work, and We Do.

A crow was sitting in a tree, doing nothing all day. A small rabbit saw the crow, and asked him,

"Can I also sit like you and do nothing all day long?"

The crow answered:

"Sure, why not?"

So, the rabbit sat on the ground below the crow, and rested. All of a sudden, a fox appeared, jumped on the rabbit and ate it.

Moral of the story:

To be sitting and doing nothing, you must be sitting very, very high up.

***

Yes, it pays to be our own boss in network marketing.

Today Might Not Be Their Day.

Imagine for a moment that I am a banker in the local community. You decide to call me at 7:00 a.m. to catch me before I leave for work. So you call at 7:00 a.m. and say, "Hi Big Al, we have a business opportunity meeting that I would like you to attend tonight. It will be in your area."

Since I am not a morning person, I would probably mumble something and hang up the phone. At 7:00 a.m. in the morning, I am not a prospect for anything!

A bit later I wake up, go downstairs and have breakfast. I read the morning paper and the headline says, "Massive Bank Layoffs Planned for the City."

I think, "Uh, oh, since I am a vice president at the local bank, this doesn't look good for me." So if you were to call me at 7:30 a.m. I might have responded, "Gosh, that opportunity meeting sounds really good. I will be there this evening."

In just 30 minutes, I went from being a bad prospect to a good prospect.

But maybe you didn't call me at 7:30 a.m. Maybe you decide to call me at 9:00 a.m., after I arrived at work.

Well, on my way to work that day, because it was raining, a car slides into me, totally demolishing my automobile. And I'm thinking, "Oh, this is terrible! Police reports, insurance problems, the car is demolished, I am going to have to buy a new car, and it is going to be a long, long walk to work."

So I walk to work in the rain, arrive soaking wet, and the phone rings. You say, "Hey Big Al, there is an opportunity meeting tonight at 8:00 p.m. Why don't you come down and check it out?'"

Talk about bad timing! I say, "No, I'm not interested. I have other things on my mind, I will talk to you later."

So at 9:00 a.m. I would not have been a good prospect for your business.

But what would have happened if you had called me at 9:30 a.m.?

Well, at 9:25 a.m. the president of the bank comes to my desk and says, "Big Al, I have some good news and I have some bad news. The bad news, Big Al, is that you are fired. We have massive bank layoffs, so you are gone. And of course the good news is that you have the rest of the day off."

Well, I'm starting to pack the things in my desk at 9:30 a.m. and you call and say, "Big Al, there is an opportunity meeting tonight at 8:00 p.m. Can you come?"

I reply, "Sounds great. I am interested. In fact, I can come and meet you right now!"

***

And that is life. Not every minute of every day is a good time for our prospects.

In just two and a half hours I went from being a bad prospect, to a good prospect, to a bad prospect and then to a good prospect.

So be patient. Allow prospects to check out your opportunity when the timing is right for them.

Taking Action.

The flood continued to get worse. The water rose from the riverbanks and demolished the town. On the outskirts of town, on high ground, lived Darrell.

Would the floodwaters reach Darrell's house? Should he sandbag the perimeter? "No need to worry," said Darrell, "I'll say a prayer and ask for God's protection. I'm sure everything will be all right."

The waters continued to rise. Soon, water covered the first floor of the house. Darrell simply went upstairs and stared out the window.

A boat floated by with the civil defense rescue team. "Hey Darrell, need a ride to safety? The flood is getting worse."

"No problem," said Darrell. "I'm on high ground, plus I said a prayer. Just go on without me. I'll be all right."

The flood did get worse. The water filled the second story, so he climbed onto the roof. Darrell said another quick prayer asking for God's protection.

A helicopter flew over the house. The pilot yelled through the loudspeaker, "Darrell! Climb up into my helicopter. The flood is getting worse."

"Don't worry about me. I've got things under control." As the helicopter flew away, the floodwaters continued to rise.

Soon the water was up to Darrell's neck, then over his head, and then it was over. Darrell perished in the flood.

Darrell led a good life, so it was no surprise that he went straight to heaven. Saint Peter gave him the grand tour and introduced him to God.

"You know, God, heaven's great," Darrell said, "but I didn't want to get here so fast. I still wanted to do some good works on earth, but then that flood came. I used to think you were a great guy and listened to my prayers, but after that flood wiped me out, I wonder. Don't you listen to the prayers of your faithful on earth? Don't you remember me asking you for safety?"

God replied, "Hey, I sent a helicopter and a boat."

***

And the point of the story?

Nothing happens unless we take action. So, **use** the stories in this book, or create and collect your own stories. When you use stories, good things happen.

Take action.

ABOUT THE AUTHOR

Tom "Big Al" Schreiter has 40+ years of experience in network marketing and MLM. As the author of the original "Big Al" training books in the late '70s, he has continued to speak in over 80 countries on using the exact words and phrases to get prospects to open up their minds and say "YES."

His passion is marketing ideas, marketing campaigns, and how to speak to the subconscious mind in simplified, practical ways. He is always looking for case studies of incredible marketing campaigns that give usable lessons.

As the author of numerous audio trainings, Tom is a favorite speaker at company conventions and regional events.

Visit Tom's blog for a regular update of network marketing and MLM business-building ideas.

http://www.BigAlBlog.com

Anyone can subscribe to his free weekly tips at:

http://www.BigAlReport.com

Made in the USA
San Bernardino, CA
30 January 2014